JUL 2006

WITHDRAWN

D0934484

HEROES OF AMERICAN HISTORY

Pocahontas
American Indian Princess

Carin T. Ford

Enslow Elementary
an imprint of

Enslow Publishers, Inc.
40 Industrial Road
Box 398
Berkeley Heights, NJ 07922
USA

http://www.enslow.com

Enslow Elementary, an imprint of Enslow Publishers, Inc.

Enslow Elementary® is a registered trademark of Enslow Publishers, Inc.

Copyright © 2006 by Enslow Publishers, Inc.

Library of Congress Cataloging-in-Publication Data

Ford, Carin T.
  Pocahontas : American Indian princess / Carin T. Ford.
    p. cm. — (Heroes of American history)
  Includes bibliographical references and index.
  ISBN 0-7660-2604-3 (hardcover)
  1. Pocahontas, d. 1617—Juvenile literature. 2. Powhatan women—Biography—Juvenile
literature. 3. Powhatan Indians—Social life and customs—Juvenile literature. I. Title.
II. Series.
  E99.P85P5733 2006
  975.5'01'092—dc22
                                                                    2005019749

Printed in the United States of America

10 9 8 7 6 5 4 3 2 1

To Our Readers: We have done our best to make sure all Internet Addresses in this book were active and appropriate when we went to press. However, the author and the publisher have no control over and assume no liability for the material available on those Internet sites or on other Web sites they may link to. Any comments or suggestions can be sent by e-mail to comments@enslow.com or to the address on the back cover.

Every effort has been made to locate all copyright holders of material used in this book. If any errors or omissions have occurred, corrections will be made in future editions of this book.

Table of Contents

Pocahontas

Chapter 1

A Daughter
of Powhatan

Pocahontas was an Indian princess. Her father, Chief Powhatan, was the leader of about thirty Powhatan Indian tribes. They lived in the area that is now Virginia, Maryland, and Delaware.

Powhatan had many children, but Pocohantas was his favorite. She was born around 1595 in Virginia. Her name was Matoaka, but everyone called her by the nickname Pocahontas—which

Powhatan Indians grew crops in their villages.

means "playful" or "naughty one." Little is known about her childhood years.

The Powhatan Indians were farmers. The women grew corn, squash, beans, and other crops. The men fished in the bay and hunted deer and turkeys in the woods. The children also had to work. They gathered firewood, helped make animal skins into clothing, carried water, and worked in the garden. For fun, they could explore the forest and swim in the river.

Most Powhatan Indians lived in wigwams,

which were small round houses. Chief Powhatan lived in a longhouse. It had a wooden frame that was covered with bark. In every village there was a council house, where leaders of the tribe met. Each village also had a building for storing food. Some villages were surrounded by logs to protect them from attack.

Using two stones, corn can be ground into corn meal for cooking.

Chief Powhatan lived in a longhouse like this.

At that time, only Indians lived in North America. People in Europe were curious about this land, which they called the New World. One day in the spring of 1607, three English ships—*Susan Constant*, *Godspeed*, and *Discovery*—sailed across the Atlantic Ocean. The men onboard were hoping to find gold.

They did not find gold. But they did set up an English colony—an area in the New World that

Hard times were ahead for the first Jamestown settlers.

would be ruled by England. They named their colony Jamestown, after King James I of England.

For Pocahontas and the rest of the Powhatan Indians, life would never be the same.

Chapter 2

Pocahontas and John Smith

J ohn Smith had sailed to the New World on the *Susan Constant*. In Jamestown, he was chosen to be one of the leaders of the colony. Right away, the settlers got busy building a fort. It was shaped like a triangle with guns at each corner.

Many of the Powhatan Indians did not trust the new settlers. They remembered that men had come from Europe in the past and killed many Indians.

They believed Englishmen were bad. Sometimes these Indians attacked the fort or shot arrows at Englishmen hunting for food in the woods.

Other Indians were curious about the English settlers. They brought food and furs to trade for small items from England.

Captain John Smith

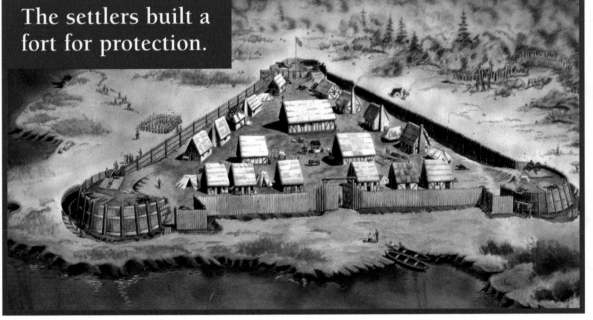

The settlers built a fort for protection.

The settlers and the Indians were
often fighting against one another.

Pocahontas was only about twelve years old. She was friendly to the settlers. She brought them food as winter drew near. She played with the boys at the fort, running around with them and turning cartwheels for fun.

As the weather grew colder, the settlers did not have enough to eat. One day, when Smith went off to find food, he was captured by Indians. They took him to Chief Powhatan, father of Pocahontas. Many years later, Smith wrote a book about his life. In his book, he told a story about the time he was captured. It was about Pocahontas. People loved this story and told it over and over until it became a part of American history. But it is likely just a legend, a story from long ago that is not really true.

John Smith met Powhatan Indians in the New World.

This is Smith's story: Powhatan wore a long robe made of raccoon fur with the tails hanging from it. Around his neck, he wore necklaces made of pearls. The room was filled with Indian men and women, including Pocahontas. Members of the tribe served a large feast. Powhatan was very interested in looking at Smith's compass. He also asked Smith many questions about the Jamestown colony.

Suddenly, Smith was grabbed by two Indian men. He was forced to lie down on a large block of stone. The guards raised their wooden clubs over Smith's head. Smith was sure they were going to kill him.

At that moment, Pocahontas ran over to Smith. She threw herself on top of him. She held his head in her arms to protect him. Powhatan told the guards

This painting illustrates the legend of Pocahontas.

to lower their clubs. He said that Smith was now his friend and would become a member of the tribe. A couple of days passed, and Smith was allowed to return to Jamestown.

After that, Pocahontas visited Jamestown many times. She and Smith became friends.

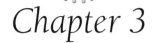
Struggles at Jamestown

L ife at Jamestown was hard. The colony was struggling to survive. Many settlers died from illness or hunger. Pocahontas often brought food to help the settlers. She also carried messages from her father. Still, there was fighting. The English wanted the Indians' land and food. The Indians wanted the English to go home. Would the settlers and the Indians ever make peace?

Sometimes English ships arrived with more

settlers. Powhatan watched Jamestown grow. He worried that the growing number of settlers meant trouble for the Indians. In 1609, Smith was badly burned when a bag of gunpowder caught fire. He had to leave Jamestown and sail for England, so doctors could take care of him. When Pocahontas visited the fort, the settlers told her that Smith was dead. She did not go back to Jamestown for four years. Some records show that

This is a copy of a house in Jamestown.

during this time Pocahontas married—and then divorced—a warrior named Kocoum. No one knows for sure if this is true.

Jamestown continued to struggle. In just six months, more than four hundred settlers died. Most of them starved to death; the others died of sicknesses. When only about sixty people were left, they decided to give up and go back to England. Then an English ship arrived. It was full of food and other supplies. The settlers stayed in Jamestown. Slowly, the colony grew.

Settlers began to lose hope during the "Starving Time."

In 1610, ships full of food and supplies arrived
just in time to save the Jamestown settlers.

Many artists have created paintings of Pocahontas.

Chapter 4

Lady Rebecca

When Pocahontas was about eighteen, she was captured by an English ship captain named Samuel Argall. He told Chief Powhatan that he wanted to make a deal. Argall would let Pocahontas go free. But Powhatan must let his English prisoners go and give back the weapons and tools taken by the Indians.

Powhatan freed the prisoners, but he did not return all the weapons. Pocahontas was not set free,

When Pocahontas was baptized
she took a new name, Rebecca.

but she was treated well by the English settlers.

Pocahontas was being kept in a village called Henrico. There, she learned the language and customs of the English people. She began to dress and act like them. Instead of wearing short skirts made of deerskin, Pocahontas now wore long English dresses. She learned about the Christian religion and was given the English name Rebecca.

A man named John Rolfe helped teach Pocahontas the English way of life. Rolfe had arrived in Jamestown in 1610. He was interested in growing tobacco. In years to come, his tobacco crops would bring a lot of money to Virginia.

John Rolfe fell in love with Pocahontas. With her long dark hair, brown skin, and dark eyes, she did not look like the other English ladies.

They were married in April 1614. At the wedding, Pocahontas wore an English wedding gown and a pearl necklace from her father. The couple built a house north of Jamestown on a plantation they called Varina. The following year, they had a son and named him Thomas.

Pocahontas with her son, Thomas.

Chapter 5

An Indian Princess in England

I n 1616, Pocahontas and her family sailed for London, England. About twelve Powhatan men and women also went on the journey.

London was very different from Virginia. The Indians were amazed by what they saw. The city was crowded with people and horses and carts. Shops were everywhere, selling food, wine, clothes, and medicines. The streets were lined with houses.

Pocahontas loved England, but the smoky air hurt her lungs.

Pocahontas was treated very well in England. She went to plays and dances and was honored to meet King James I.

Pocahontas was surprised when she learned that Captain John Smith was not dead. He was living in England. Smith wrote a letter to Queen Anne. He said Pocahontas had been very kind to the Jamestown settlers.

Pocahontas had been in England for just seven months when her husband

King James I.

Pocahontas met the king of England.

decided to sail back to Virginia. He needed to take care of his tobacco business.

Pocahontas had not been feeling well for a while. She had an illness in her lungs. In March 1617, she boarded a ship that was heading for Virginia. Yet she was too sick to make the journey. The ship had to dock at Gravesend, England. There, Pocahontas was taken ashore.

Ætatis suæ 21. Aº. 1616.

Pocahontas dressed like an Englishwoman.

Rolfe stayed by her side as she lay dying. She told him, "All must die. 'Tis enough that the child liveth."

Pocahontas died later that same month at Gravesend and was buried at St. George's Parish Church. She was twenty-two years old.

Her son, Thomas, went to school in England. Later, he moved to Virginia.

Pocahontas was an Indian princess who is remembered for helping the settlers in Jamestown, Virginia. She is a symbol of peace among people of different races.

This statue of Pocahontas stands near the original Jamestown site.

Timeline

1595~ Pocahontas is born in Virginia.

1607~ Englishmen arrive and set up the colony of Jamestown. Pocahontas meets John Smith.

1610~ May have been married for a time to Kocoum.

1613~ Is captured by the English. Takes the English name Rebecca.

1614~ Marries John Rolfe.

1615~ Has a son, Thomas.

1616~ Travels to London, England, and meets the king.

1617~ Dies on March 21 in Gravesend, England, and is buried there.

1624~ John Smith writes his story about Pocahontas.

Words to Know

baptism—To dip in or sprinkle with water as a welcome into the Christian religion.

colony—An area ruled by a faraway country.

compass—A tool for telling direction: north, south, east, and west.

historian—A person who studies history or writes about it.

New World—The name used by explorers for North America and South America.

plantation—A very large farm.

settler—A person who settles (that is, sets up his or her home) in a new area.

tobacco—A plant with large leaves that are dried for smoking.

wigwam—A rounded hut made of poles covered by bark or animal skins.

Learn More

Books

Polette, Nancy. *Pocahontas*. New York: Children's Press, 2003.

Schaefer, Lola M. *Pocahontas*. Mankato, Minn.: Pebble Books, 2002.

Williams, Suzanne. *Powhatan Indians*. Chicago: Heinemann Library, 2003.

Internet Addresses

America's Library: Meet Amazing Americans
http://www.americaslibrary.gov/cgi-bin/page.cgi/aa/pocahontas

History Globe: The Jamestown Online Adventure
http://www.historyglobe.com/jamestown/

Jamestown Rediscovery: Pocahontas
http://www.apva.org/history/pocahont.html

Index